CAPITAL ACQUISITION

Small Business Considerations

for HOW TO GET FINANCING

HENDRITH VANLON SMITH JR

© 2023 by Hendrith Vanlon Smith Jr

All rights reserved. No portion of this book may be reproduced, stored in a retrieval system or large language model,
or transmitted in any form or by any means electronic, mechanical, photocopy, recording,
scannIng, or other- except for brief quotations in critical reviews or articles, without the prior written permission of the author.

Library of Congress Cataloging-in-Publication Data
Smith Jr, Hendrith Vanlon, 1989–
Capital Acquisition: Small Business Considerations for How to Get Financing
/ Hendrith Vanlon Smith Jr

ISBN: 978-1-312-15260-1

*Superior formatting available in paperback/hardcover editions

Printed in The USA

Introduction

Every business needs capital. Whether we're talking about a barber shop or a bank, a boutique e-commerce store or a hotdog stand. Whether we're talking about a restaurant or a clothing store, a giant like Walmart, or the local bodega owned by a local family. They all need capital. The quantity of capital they need will vary of course. The timing of when they need Capital will vary. And the contexts within which they need capital will vary. But the fact that they all need capital remains constant. Because in our society, everything costs money – and it very often takes money to make money. So regardless of what kind of business you lead, you should know that you're not alone – far from it. Focus on putting yourself and your business in a position to get financing.

One important thing to consider and keep in mind is that if your business is approved for financing and designated to be a recipient of capital, it will be because your business' debt is a lenders investment and your liability is a lenders asset. Your line of business may be about how many customers come in to buy your food or the demand for construction projects in a given city, or whatever. That's how you make a living. But for lenders, their line of business is about borrowers following through on loan terms through to maturity. That's how bankers make a living.

Therefore, you should look at things from a different perspective and start asking questions like what do I need to do to make it such that lenders perceive my business as a good investment? What can I do to ensure that lenders perceive my business as an asset that will reliably yield them an income, and a profit? What can I do to make sure that my business is good for their business?

Bankers throughour time have used what we call "The Five C's of Credit' as a basis of evaluating the worthiness of a potential borrower. In this book, I guide you on a quick journey of discovery – discovering the Five C's and discovering what you can do to master each one to put yourself and your business in a great position to qualify for the capital you need or want.

This book is a simple introduction; a starting point. It does not contain any mathematical formulas or MBA level anecdotes. Nor does it contain any handholding or step-by-step procedural how-to's. It's a book of *considerations* – things for you to *consider* as a small business entrepreneur or someone interested in starting a business. Many entrepreneurs understand their line of business very well, but lack a basic awareness, or understanding of what it takes to qualify for capital, and why. I aim to address this deficit in this simple introductory book. The considerations presented in this book are simply intended to spark insight, provide context, refine mental models, and inspire action. Upon the completion of this book, heavier reading is recommended.

contents

1. Qualifying through proof of great Character

2. Qualifying through proof of great Capacity

3. Qualifying through proof of great Capital

4. Qualifying through proof of great Collateral

5. Qualifying through proof of great Conditions

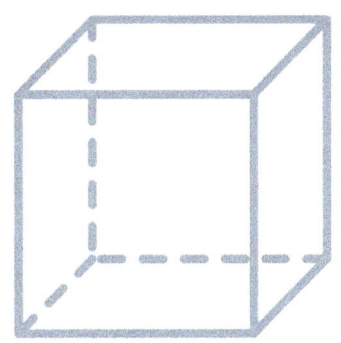 **CHARACTER**

Every lender is interested in the character of his borrowers. Ask yourself a question – would you want to lend money to somebody that you do not trust? I would be willing to bet the answer to that question, is a resounding "no." why? Well, there's a difference between alone and a charitable donation. When someone or some entity gives a charitable donation, they are most likely not expecting a financial return on that charitable donation. And even if they are expecting a financial return, the return will come in the form of a tax benefit awarded by the government, and not by the recipient of the charitable donation. The trustworthiness of the receiver will not have any bearing on the givers likelihood of receiving the tax benefit from the governor. However, when someone or some entity gives a loan, they are expecting Dash often to the point of necessity – to receive that money back, and to receive it back with interest. The more trustworthy a borrower is, the greater the likelihood that they will return the money lent to them back to the lender with interest. This is why lenders of every kind and size, place a high priority on the character of potential borrowers – it is one of the five key determining factors as to the likelihood of the lender receiving their money back with interest.

> *We all really only want to lend our money to people we can trust to pay it back. It's the same thing with banks and other institutional lenders.*

HENDRITH VANLON SMITH JR

When it comes to friends and family, you can often be easy to demonstrate your character. In all likelihood, if you are someone who does have a good character, that has been proven time and time again over the course of many years or even many decades in your relationships with these people. This is why it is often easier to borrow money from friends and family than it is to borrow money from banks and other institutional lenders. When it comes to banks and other institutional lenders, they do not know you as a person. So they have to rely on less intimate data to determine whether or not you are trustworthy and to what extent you can be trusted to repay a loan. And again it is exactly that – it's about your trustworthiness in terms of loan repayment. Lenders are not very concerned about your trustworthiness as a friend when a friend needs comfort. Lenders are not very concerned with your trustworthiness as a member of your church. Lenders are not very concerned with how well your children can rely on you, or how seriously you take your commitment to your clients. These things matter, and hopefully, in the future, we have more of an ability to factor these things in to lending decisions.

But a persons trustworthiness in one area of life may not necessarily transfer over to their trustworthiness as a borrower. And a business that can be trusted to do the right thing for its customers may not necessarily be a business that can be trusted to do the right thing for its creditors.

So, having the ability to demonstrate your character holistically is definitely meaningful. I mean if it's known that a person is a horrible friend and a horrible parent whose relationships are defined by neglect, any lender would find difficulty in viewing this person as trustworthy as a potential borrower. But in actuality, a persons or a businesses trustworthiness in terms of loan repayment does not necessarily *always* correlate to their trustworthiness in other areas of their lives – though often times it does. In the eyes of lenders, what is *most* important is your ability or your business' ability to demonstrate character relative to your likelihood of repaying a loan with interest. It's mostly about your character in terms of money. If you or your business can demonstrate character in this context, lenders will often times be uninterested in or overlook character in other contexts.

Most often this is proven by historical data or credit history – how often you've repaid previous loans, how many times you've been late to repay, how many times if ever you've defaulted on a loan, how much money have lenders lent you in the past, etc. character is not something that is viewed as a snapshot, but rather, it's some thing that is viewed as an average over a long continuum of time.

I hope moving forward lenders will begin viewing people and businesses more holistically, and judging them on the totality of their character. This will have huge implications for the allocation of capital at scale, ensuring that capital flows align with our sense of morality as a society. But for the record, I do believe that character, in terms of money has a lot to do with morality. So until then, and even when that time comes, focus on being a reliable person in terms of money and focus on, ensuring that your business is a reliable business in terms of money.

Both you and your business should be financially, trustworthy – and, you should be able to demonstrate that financial trustworthiness because this is how lenders will judge your character.

In essence, lenders are not interested in the other aspects of your life, but rather your ability to repay loans with interest. They are looking for a track record of reliability and financial trustworthiness. This means that if you have a poor credit history, lenders may see you as a high-risk borrower and deny you a loan or charge you higher interest rates. On the other hand, if you have a good credit history and have demonstrated financial responsibility in the past, lenders will be more likely to view you as a low-risk borrower and may offer you lower interest rates or higher loan amounts. It's important to remember that your character is not just viewed as a snapshot, but rather as a long continuum of time. So, focus on building a strong financial track record to demonstrate your trustworthiness to lenders.

In the realm of finance and lending, the bedrock of trust and character carries an immeasurable weight. This simple yet profound truth underscores the essence of lending and the critical importance of understanding the character of borrowers. When you consider the act of lending, it's akin to a trust-based transaction. Lenders are essentially entrusting their hard-earned resources to the care of others, with the expectation of not only the principal amount's return but also the generation of interest. In essence, lending is not charity; it's a financial partnership that hinges on trust.

So, would you, as a lender, be willing to extend your resources to someone you don't trust? The answer to this question invariably resonates with a resounding "no." Trust forms the foundation of any lending relationship, large or small. It's the catalyst for a fruitful partnership, the assurance that borrowed funds will be returned, and the incentive for the lender to participate in this financial exchange. It's this trust that transforms lending into a mutually beneficial transaction.

For lenders, the character of borrowers is a linchpin that influences the likelihood of their funds returning with interest. This pivotal character element is one of the five crucial factors that lenders meticulously evaluate to gauge the potential risk associated with the borrower. A borrower's trustworthiness holds the key to unlocking lending opportunities and securing successful financial partnerships.

In conclusion, this understanding of trust and character in lending underscores the importance of diligence and responsibility in managing financial transactions. It acts as a guiding principle for lenders, a reminder of the integral role character plays in the world of finance. Ultimately, trust is the currency that fuels lending, and character is the compass that ensures a safe and successful journey in the intricate landscape of financial transactions.

4 Things You Can do

● When starting your business, make sure the business address and phone number are likely to be constants over at least a two year time period. This information will report to credit bureaus and needs to match with current data and across bureaus. Data inconsistencies are often a cause for automatic rejection of credit.

● Have your business apply for and obtain a D-U-N-S number from Dun & Bradstreet. This D-U-N-S number in conjunction with the business's EIN, will be asked for by many lenders as a prerequisite for credit. And even if they do t require it for the extension of credit, it may be required to enable them to report your business's credit history to credit bureaus.

● Apply for ten 'Net-30' accounts in the business name. A Net-30 account is a type of credit line that allows a business to buy items from a merchant and allows them 30 days to pay for it. The business will not even get a credit report generated until it has five credit lines. Different merchants apply to doffering bureaus. So having ten should ensure that the business has reports generated for every bureau.

● Keep your personal credit in good standing and make repairs to your personal credit where necessary. Many small business lenders require a "Personal Guarantee.' This means that there has to be an actual person sign off on a business loan. If the business doesn't pay the loan, the lender will havethe right to hold the person accountable and get the money from them. As the owner, that person will most likely be you. And your personal credit report and scores could be determining factors as to whether or not your business qualifies for financing. Sidenote of equal value: When possible, do NOT mix your personal finances with your business finances. It's generally a horrible idea. But when a business is new and small and does not have a track record of its own, lenders will often require a personal guarantee.

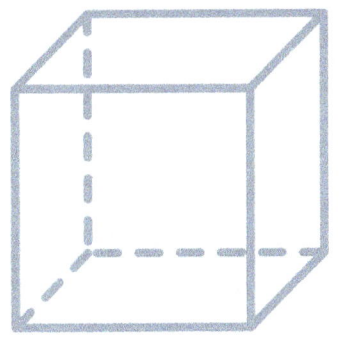

CAPACITY

Whereas character is about a borrowers sense of morality and their behavioral history in a financial context, capacity is about the borrowers *ability* to repay a loan. Theoretically, and as has been the case for many borrowers who have defaulted on their loans, a borrower may have a strong desire and commitment to repay a loan yet lack the actual ability to repay it. And this is why capacity is just as important as character when it comes to capital acquisition.

Let's consider an example – if you lend money to an honest priest to start an ice cream stand in Antarctica, I regret to inform you that you probably will not get your money back if repayment is up to the profitability of that business. We have a theoretical priest who is honest – he's someone you can trust – He's a good person. But an ice cream stand in Antarctica is probably a bad idea as a business. Therefore this hypothetical borrower has the character, but does not have the capacity. As a lender, I would most certainly request a personal guarantee from this priest turned businessman, requiring him to personally repay the loan, because quite honestly, I have no faith in the businesses ability to do so. If the priest does not qualify to give a personal guarantee, I will not finance the business at all – viewing the arrangement as too risky – and the likelihood of default, too high.

> *Trustworthiness is one thing. Being **able** to pay the money back is another.*

HENDRITH VANLON SMITH JR

The notable Debt-To-Income ratio is the standard formula most lenders use to determine a potential borrowers capacity. Lenders calculate this by adding up a borrower's total monthly debt payments and dividing that by the borrowers gross monthly income. A borrower that has a low DTI ratio has a better chance of qualifying for a new loan. Whereas a borrower with a higher DTI ratio has a worst chance of qualify for a new loan. The basic premise is that if a borrower can barely afford to pay their current expenses, they will definitely not be able to afford incurring any additional expenses – especially as a continuous commitment.

It's important to note that the Debt-To-Income ratio is not the only factor that lenders consider when evaluating a borrower's creditworthiness. Other factors like credit score, employment history, and savings are also taken into account. However, having a low DTI ratio is certainly a positive indicator that a borrower is financially responsible and capable of taking on additional debt. It's also worth mentioning that a high DTI ratio doesn't necessarily mean that a borrower is irresponsible or unable to pay their debts. Lenders may take into account things like the borrower's job stability or the potential for future income growth. Ultimately, it's up to the lender to decide whether or not to approve a loan application based on a number of different factors, including the borrower's DTI ratio.

When businesses, face hardships, there tend to be a certain priority arrangement, in terms of who to pay first, and which obligations should warrant the most commitment. Business is due this the same way people do this. I would be willing to bet that if you personally were low on money, you will choose to feed yourself and your family before you pay for your streaming subscriptions. I would be willing to bet that if you had to ever choose between paying your basic housing expenses or paying your credit card bill, you will probably choose the former above the latter.

To go, even deeper, if you ever had to choose between your mortgage, which is a loan and paying your credit card, which is also a loan – I'd be willing to bet you would choose to pay your mortgage as the loan with greater priority. I guess it boils down to Maslow's hierarchy of needs. Your mortgage represents immediate needs, and more significant needs, whereas your credit card does not. Lenders tend to know where they stand in all of this. Lenders are not naïve enough to believe that in the event of financial crisis, you would use to honor that your commitment to them ahead of your commitment to things that may represent more urgent need.

The same is true for businesses. A business is just a collection of people making decisions on behalf of the business, and those people tend to subject the business to the same kind of priority arrangements – with things like payroll and rent and electricity, being considered as more important than a business credit card bill. This presents an added layer of risk to lenders that they must account for in the terms of any potential loan. As a borrower, you want to be able to prove that you have so much capacity that you would never have to make such choices. You want to be able to prove that you have so much capacity that you can meet all of your commitments with ease, and even have enough capacity leftover to take on new commitments and meet those new commitments with ease as well.

4 Things You Can do

- Reduce your businesses monthly expenses. This is where you will likely find the most opportunity to reduce the business' DTI ratio. If you can cut expenses by say 10% or 15% even, it could mean the difference between a rejection and an approval of financing.

- Increase your business' income. Sometimes Businesssometimes business owners willingly forfeit income, simply because they don't want to do the things that are necessary to get that additional income. Opening later hours is a good example. But opening for an additional two hours a day for a consistent six months could result in the business having the additional income needed to increase the DTI.

- Refinance existing debt, so as to have the effect that even with an equivalent total debt outstanding, the interest rate and the required monthly payments on the debt have been reduced.

- Solicit co-signers or business partners who have superior capacity. Ask them to back the request for financing along with you or the business – perhaps in exchange for equity or something else they deem valuable.

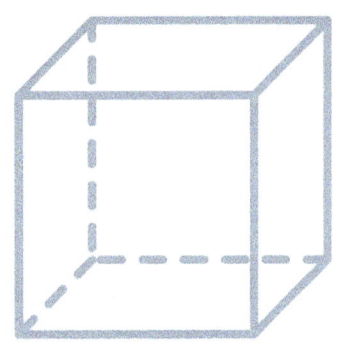
CAPITAL

Let's start with a quote from the Bible. In the book of Matthew 25-29, it says "For to everyone who has will be given, and he will have abundance. But from him who has not even that which he has will be taken away." The reality is that wealth attracts wealth and money goes where money is.

Let's observe a hypothetical scenario with a large company like Walmart. We're not talking about Walmart specifically, we're just talking about a large company like Walmart — company that earns hundreds of millions or billions of dollars annually in revenues. Will call this company XYZ corporation. Let's say XYZ corporation has $100 million in an investment portfolio which is expected to yield a 10% annual return resulting in an additional $10 million. Let's say after taxes that $10 million is reduced to $6 million. Haven't been earned at the end of one year. Let's say this year revenues for XYZ corporation are expected to be less than revenues for the recent previous years and XYZ corporation needs to somehow bridge the gap between their constant expenses, and their forecasted decrease in Revenues. And let's say the difference between the two just happens to be $100 million. Well, XYZ cooperation could simply withdraw the $100 million from their investment portfolio and use that bridge the gap.

Or, XYZ corporation could borrow $100 million from a lender. Let's say that a lender is willing to lend XYZ corporation $100 million at a 4% interest rate resulting in XYZ corporation having repaid $100 million in principle plus $4 million in interest at the end of one year to the lender. Do you see where this is going? If XYZ corporation withdraws the $100 million from there portfolio, it will be in effect forfeiting a $6 million gain to avoid a $4 million interest expense. It would make more sense financially to borrow $100 million at 4% then to withdraw the $100 million from their portfolio. In this scenario, it's not a matter of the borrower, not having the money. It's a matter of fact that borrowing the money is less costly than spending the money that they have. These tends to be the best case scenarios for both borrowers and lenders. This is a common financial strategy used by corporations and individuals alike. By borrowing money at a lower interest rate than the return they expect to earn on their investment portfolio, they can effectively make a profit. Of course, this strategy does come with risks. If the investments don't perform as expected, the borrower could end up owing more than they earned, resulting in a net loss. It's important to carefully consider the potential risks and rewards before pursuing this strategy, and to work with a financial advisor to ensure that it's the right choice for your unique situation.

> *It's ironic perhaps — but no one wants to lend money to someone or something that has no money or no monetary worth.*

HENDRITH VANLON SMITH JR

The principle that "money goes where money is" underscores a fundamental reality in the world of finance. It's a concept rooted in the dynamics of capital and wealth growth that has far-reaching implications for individuals, corporations, and the broader economy.

Let's explore this concept further through a real-world lens. In the business world, thriving companies often accumulate substantial wealth through profitable operations, investments, or other financial ventures. This wealth can take the form of liquid assets, equities, or interest-bearing investments. What's remarkable is that once a business has amassed a significant financial resource base, it opens the doors to even more financial opportunities.

The hypothetical scenario featuring XYZ Corporation, representative of many established entities, offers a striking illustration of this dynamic. XYZ Corporation's $100 million investment portfolio, expected to yield a 10% annual return, is a testament to their financial prowess. However, as the saying goes, "money begets money," which is why XYZ Corporation is both wealthy and astute. They are poised to earn an additional $10 million, which, after taxes, amounts to $6 million by year-end.

But here's the twist. Despite having $100 million readily available, XYZ Corporation faces a challenge: their projected revenues for the current year are anticipated to fall short, creating a $100 million gap between expected income and consistent expenses. In response, they have two options. They could withdraw the $100 million from their investment portfolio, essentially tapping into their vast resources, or they could opt to borrow the same amount from a lender.

What makes this scenario so intriguing is that borrowing, which is typically associated with a financial deficit, is, in this case, the more cost-effective choice. XYZ Corporation could secure a $100 million loan at a 4% interest rate, meaning they would repay the principal and an additional $4 million in interest after one year. When viewed from a financial perspective, borrowing is the prudent choice, as it allows them to preserve their $6 million investment gain while incurring only a $4 million interest cost.

This scenario is not an isolated incident; it's a reflection of a broader financial principle. Wealthy individuals and businesses understand that financial decisions should be based on optimizing returns and minimizing costs.

The ability to recognize the advantages of borrowing over spending existing capital is a hallmark of financial shrewdness. It's a reminder that having access to substantial resources is valuable, but the manner in which those resources are managed can make all the difference.

Beyond the corporate sphere, this principle extends to individual financial decisions. Whether it's managing personal investments, considering mortgages, or assessing student loans, the concept holds true. Smart financial choices can lead to wealth preservation and growth.

In conclusion, the notion that "money goes where money is" transcends financial transactions. It embodies the wisdom of leveraging resources effectively to generate wealth and prosperity. This principle should guide individuals and businesses in their financial endeavors. Ultimately, it's a reminder that in the realm of finance, strategic choices are often more valuable than sheer wealth. The ability to discern when to utilize existing capital and when to borrow or invest is a skill that can significantly impact financial success and longevity.

Whether you're an executive, an entrepreneur or an employee with stewardship over a company's finances; here are a few things you can do for the company along these lines.

1. Leverage Existing Capital Efficiently: Business leaders should take a page from the concept of "money goes where money is" by assessing their available resources and investments. Just as XYZ Corporation made a savvy choice to borrow instead of depleting their investment portfolio, business leaders should evaluate if borrowing, lending, or reinvesting in the business can lead to higher returns or cost savings. Decisions should be driven by a thorough analysis of which option is more financially advantageous, balancing risks and benefits.

2. Financial Strategy Planning: Entrepreneurs and executives should develop robust financial strategies that align with their business goals. These strategies should include contingencies for potential financial gaps, market fluctuations, and risk management. By having a clear financial plan in place, businesses can make informed decisions regarding the allocation of resources, investments, and borrowings..

3. Optimize Investment Returns: The ability to grow wealth lies not only in accumulating capital but also in optimizing returns on investments. Leaders should actively manage their portfolios, diversify investments, and explore opportunities for growth while keeping an eye on market trends. Just as XYZ Corporation aimed for a 10% annual return, businesses should seek out avenues that provide the best return on investment.

4. Consider Borrowing Wisely: Borrowing is a strategic tool for business growth. Entrepreneurs can access capital to expand their operations, launch new products or services, or seize market opportunities. However, borrowing should be done prudently, with careful consideration of interest rates, terms, and the potential return on investment. When borrowing results in a net gain, it can be a more sensible choice than depleting existing assets.

5. Continuous Learning and Analysis: In a dynamic financial landscape, it's crucial for business leaders to stay informed about economic trends, financial markets, and the implications of different financial decisions. Regularly reviewing financial strategies and investments is vital. This practice enables business leaders to adapt to changing conditions and seize opportunities that can boost their financial health.

6. Seek Financial Expertise: It's advisable for business leaders to consult with financial experts, advisors, and professionals. These experts can provide valuable insights and help assess the financial implications of various decisions. Whether it's a tax advisor, investment consultant, or financial planner, their guidance can play a vital role in optimizing financial strategies.

7. Manage Debt Responsibly: Borrowing should be managed responsibly, ensuring that it aligns with the company's overall financial health. Business leaders should consider the impact of debt on the balance sheet and cash flow and weigh this against the potential benefits of leveraging borrowed funds.

8. Risk Mitigation: Business leaders should be diligent in assessing financial risks associated with their decisions. This includes evaluating the stability of investments, interest rate changes, and market volatility. By taking steps to mitigate risks, companies can safeguard their financial stability.

In summary, the principle that "money goes where money is" underscores the importance of making strategic financial choices that maximize returns and minimize costs. Business leaders and entrepreneurs should apply these recommendations to optimize their financial strategies and grow their wealth effectively, ensuring long-term financial success and resilience.

4 Things You Can do

 Make sure your business has a business savings account with automatic transfers set up from the business checking to the business savings. Treat this with as much priority as your business rent or electric bill. In time, the business will have its own store of capital.

 If possible and feasible, try to on the space where your business is, operating as opposed to renting it. There may be times when owning the space is not ideal and where it is actually better to rent, but owning the space does at least mean that the business has an additional kind of capital on its books.

 Look around within the business at what can be turned into capital. For example, if you own a restaurant with a very popular sauce, look into securing a patent on that sauce recipe. That patent is a kind of capital and gives the business as an added layer of worth.

 Evaluate and improve on the goodwill of the business, and put that in to financial terms. Brand recognition, followers on social media, and customer loyalty are examples of goodwill. They can be hard to quantify, and are often quantified at a discount, but nonetheless, they are a form of non-financial capital that can be translated into financial capital.

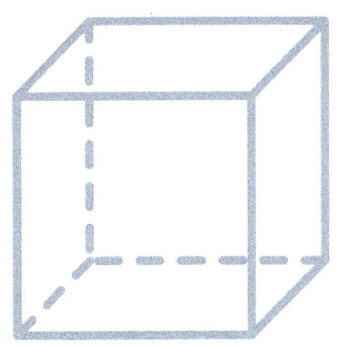 **COLLATERAL**

Remember, every lender is concerned with getting their principal (the money they loaned) back along with interest (their profit). Think about it – you are a businessman or a businesswoman and do you want to sell anything or provide any service and not get a profit? No. Lenders are the same. Lenders are also business men and women. But their business is financing other businesses. And they must make a profit on that somehow, otherwise they won't be in business very long. They just want to make sure that they're getting their money back along with a Profit. And that's really what every business wants to do.

Collateral is one way that lenders give themselves greater assurance on this. In the event that a business is unable or unwilling to repay a loan, the lender wants to have a legal right to take something of value away from the borrower, so that it can be sold to reclaim however much money was lent or more. In most cases, lenders are not interested in owning the collateral itself – they are only interested in the cash value of the collateral.

> *Lenders want to have peace of mind when it comes to getting their money back plus profit — collateral is one thing that gives that peace of mind.*

HENDRITH VANLON SMITH JR

Think about this for a moment. If you lend someone $10,000, and they do not pay it back then you lost $10,000 right? Well that's partially right. Yes you lost $10,000, but you also lost in much more than that. You could have invested that $10,000 into the markets and if you earned a 4% return on that $10,000, you would have earned a $400 profit. So arguably you lost at least $10,400 on the default loan. If you had secured the rights to a food cart that the barber owned which has a market value of $7000, in the event of default you could secure that food cart and sell it for $7000 at which point you would have only lost $3400 as opposed to $10,400. This is why collateral is often times so important. Some people in their ignorance view collateral securing as wrong – as a kind of theft even. But for the lender, there is nothing glorious about it. It's not a win for the lender when they take that collateral from the borrower. Lenders are not in the retail business – they're not interested in selling things and furthermore they lack the capacity to engage in retail selling competitively. If it gets to the point where collateral must be secured, it is often times about the lender taking a smaller loss as opposed to a bigger loss. Collateral is really about minimizing the L

The adage "money goes where money is" holds true in the world of financing and lending, and one of the key factors that lenders assess is the presence of collateral or assets that can be used as capital. This principle emphasizes the significance of having tangible assets as a way to gain approval for financing. Let's delve into the importance of assets and collateral in the world of business and lending.

Lenders, just like businesspeople, are driven by the goal of earning a profit. When lending money, they aim to recoup the principal amount along with interest, which constitutes their earnings. Lenders are essentially business entities specializing in the finance sector. Their success relies on the prudent allocation of their capital to borrowers who will fulfill their financial obligations.

Collateral serves as an essential tool that provides lenders with greater confidence in the lending process. In the unfortunate event that a borrower cannot or will not repay a loan, lenders require the legal right to seize an asset of value from the borrower. This asset, in most cases, is not something that lenders aim to possess or use themselves; instead, they are interested in its cash value. Collateral ensures that lenders can recover the amount lent or even more, protecting their financial interests.

The concept of collateral becomes especially clear when considering the true cost of a defaulting loan. If a lender extends a loan of $10,000, and the borrower defaults, the lender doesn't merely lose the principal amount. They also lose the potential profits that could have been generated from that capital. In this case, if the lender could have invested that $10,000 at a 4% return, they would have earned an additional $400 profit. Therefore, the real loss extends beyond the principal amount, potentially encompassing both the borrowed sum and the missed opportunity for profit.

Collateral emerges as a safeguard in this context. By obtaining collateral, the lender secures an additional asset of equivalent or near-equivalent value to the loan. In the event of a default, the lender can claim this collateral and sell it to recover the outstanding balance. This not only minimizes their loss but also mitigates the risk associated with lending.

Critics of collateral might view it as unjust or even as a form of theft. However, for lenders, collateral is not a desirable outcome. They do not wish to own or sell the collateral; their primary objective is to ensure they can recover the lent amount or more in case of a default.

It's not about winning or profiting from the borrower's assets; it's about protecting their own interests and reducing potential losses.

In summary, collateral and tangible assets play a pivotal role in the lending process. They offer lenders security and assurance, reducing their risk of loss in case of loan default. Business leaders, entrepreneurs, and individuals seeking financing should consider the importance of collateral when approaching lenders, as it can increase the likelihood of loan approval and provide a safeguard for both parties involved in the financial transaction.

Collateral holds immense importance to lenders for several compelling reasons:

1. Risk Mitigation: Lending inherently carries a level of risk. Lenders, whether they are banks, financial institutions, or individuals, aim to reduce this risk. Collateral provides a safeguard against potential losses, as it offers a tangible asset that can be liquidated if the borrower defaults. This significantly lowers the lender's exposure to financial risk.

2. Asset Liquidity: Collateral, in the form of tangible assets like real estate, vehicles, or valuable inventory, has a known market value. This liquidity allows lenders to recover their funds swiftly by selling the collateral, ensuring they can recoup the lent amount without a prolonged and costly legal process.

3. Risk Assessment: Collateral enhances the lender's ability to assess the creditworthiness of the borrower. It indicates that the borrower is willing to put their valuable assets at stake, which suggests a higher level of commitment and responsibility. This can lead to more favorable loan terms, such as lower interest rates or larger loan amounts.

4. Debt Recovery: In cases of loan default, collateral serves as a clear mechanism for lenders to recover their funds. Rather than relying solely on legal proceedings or chasing after the borrower, the lender can seize and sell the collateral, streamlining the debt recovery process and reducing the associated costs.

5. Asset Value Assurance: By obtaining collateral, lenders can ensure that the value of the assets is sufficient to cover the loan amount.

This minimizes uncertainty and the risk of suffering losses. It allows lenders to have greater confidence that they will not incur substantial financial setbacks even if the borrower defaults.

6. Widening Borrowing Opportunities: Collateral provides borrowers with the means to access financing they might not otherwise qualify for. Lenders are often more willing to approve loans, even for individuals or businesses with less-than-perfect credit, if they have valuable collateral to secure the loan.

7. Lower Interest Rates: Collateral-backed loans are generally perceived as less risky by lenders. In such cases, borrowers may enjoy lower interest rates because the reduced risk translates to a lower cost of borrowing. This can save borrowers significant amounts of money over the life of a loan.

In essence, collateral plays a pivotal role in the relationship between lenders and borrowers. It provides a sense of security for lenders, ensuring that they can minimize losses if things do not go as planned.

For borrowers, collateral can open up access to financing opportunities and potentially more favorable loan terms. As a result, collateral is considered an essential element in the world of lending, offering a win-win solution for both lenders and borrowers.

In essence, collateral plays a pivotal role in the relationship between lenders and borrowers. It provides a sense of security for lenders, ensuring that they can minimize losses if things do not go as planned. For borrowers, collateral can open up access to financing opportunities and potentially more favorable loan terms. As a result, collateral is considered an essential element in the world of lending, offering a win-win solution for both lenders and borrowers.

4 Things You Can do

- Acquire assets in the business name. That could include real estate property, stocks, equipment, Intellectual Property, etc. While it's often times good for the business to own these kinds of assets, simply, for its own sake – another reason is that these may serve as collateral if necessary.

- Make sure the business has the title to whatever you intend to use as collateral. If another party has rights to whatever asset you think you can use as collateral, you may be incorrect in the matter. It may be the case that that thing cannot be used as collateral at all or that the value of that thing as collateral is significantly reduced. In other words, nothing that has a lien on it.

- Keep an organized file of documents that prove ownership. Lenders will need verification that the business actually owns what it says it owns. The lender will need this not only as proof of the businesses, integrity, but should it ever get to the point where collateral needs to be secured, the lender will need those documents. If For Business cannot provide these documents or ownership cannot be verified by a third-party like a government data collector, it likely cannot be collateralized.

- Have a lawyer do an Asset review for your business. I have discovered that lawyers are very clever individuals and will likely discover options for your business and you did not know we're available.

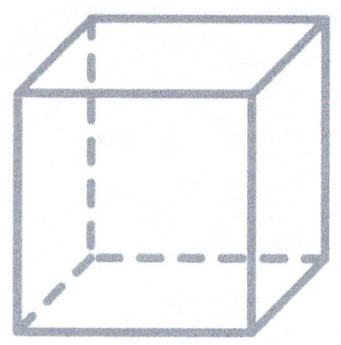

CONDITIONS

Conditions is the one C of the five C's that borrowers have the least control of. But it should still be something that borrowers consider, and account for.

Conditions may include things that are specific to the possible loan, such as the requested amount of the loan, which, from the lender's perspective is the principle, or the interest rate at which the lender can feasibly issue the loan. Another condition could be how the borrower intends to utilize the loan. What the loan will be used for can have significant implications as to the likelihood of repayment and the likelihood of default. As a borrower, you want to make sure that you are requesting an amount that the business can realistically repay along with interest. Now this may not necessarily be limited to present income, though it often is and often should be. But in many cases, a business is seeking broad expansion, and can prove to a large extent that the expansion will result in greater capacity to repay the loan. Under this condition, the lender may still be likely to approve financing for the borrower.

Conditions may include information that is far out of the borrowers control – such as how the industry the business exists in is performing as a whole.

> *There's a best time for everything – including the acquisition of capital.*

HENDRITH VANLON SMITH JR

You could also include the condition of the state economy, or the national economy as a whole. or the presumed legislative changes likely to arise now that a new political party has been elected. While you, as the borrower have no control over these kinds of conditions, it is important to keep them in mind. They can serve as indicators or guideposts to borrowers as to when is a great time to seek financing and when is a bad time to seek financing. With careful observation of these kind of macro conditions, entrepreneurs can become somewhat attuned to when capital will be broadly available, and position themselves to get it – and when capital will be broadly, restricted, and make sure that they will not be needing additional capital during such times.

The "Conditions" aspect of the Five C's of credit plays a critical role in the approval or rejection of business financing. Although borrowers may have limited control over certain external conditions, it is essential to understand and consider these factors when seeking loans or credit for their businesses. Here, we delve into the significance of "Conditions" and how it can influence the financing landscape.

1. Loan Amount and Interest Rates: One of the primary conditions is the loan amount requested and the interest rate at which the loan can be issued. From a lender's perspective, the principle amount and interest rate are key determinants of the risk associated with the loan. Borrowers should be cautious not to overextend themselves by requesting an amount that their business cannot realistically repay along with interest. Prudent financial planning aligns the requested amount with the business's capacity to service the debt.

2. Loan Purpose: The purpose for which the loan will be used can have a significant impact on loan approval. Lenders are interested in understanding how the funds will be utilized. A business expansion plan that demonstrates the potential for increased income and repayment capacity is more likely to receive approval. Clear and well-defined business goals for the loan proceeds can positively influence lending decisions.

3. Industry Performance and Economic Conditions: Some conditions are beyond a borrower's control, such as the performance of the industry in which their business operates or the state of the national economy.

Broader economic and industry conditions can significantly affect the availability and terms of financing. Borrowers must keep a watchful eye on these macro-level indicators to gauge the timing for seeking capital. Being attuned to when capital is readily available and when it might be restricted can help businesses make more informed financing decisions.

4. Governmental and Legislative Changes: Changes in the political landscape can bring about legislative shifts that affect the business environment. These changes can impact lending conditions and the overall business climate. Entrepreneurs should remain aware of potential regulatory alterations and plan their financing needs accordingly. Staying informed about legislative changes can help businesses adapt and ensure they do not require additional capital during uncertain or unfavorable periods.

5. Cyclical Business Factors: Some businesses are influenced by seasonal or cyclical factors. Understanding these industry-specific conditions is essential when seeking financing. Lenders may be more willing to accommodate these fluctuations if borrowers can demonstrate a clear strategy for managing the cyclical nature of their business.

In summary, while borrowers may not have direct control over certain conditions, they should consider and account for these factors when seeking financing. By aligning their loan requests with their business's capacity to repay, understanding the broader economic and industry landscape, and staying informed about legislative changes, entrepreneurs can increase their chances of securing financing on favorable terms. Ultimately, being attentive to conditions as part of the Five C's of credit can help businesses make more informed and strategic financing decisions.

4 Things You Can do

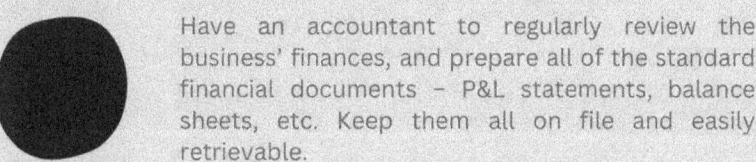 Have an accountant to regularly review the business' finances, and prepare all of the standard financial documents – P&L statements, balance sheets, etc. Keep them all on file and easily retrievable.

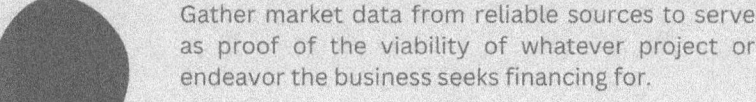 Gather market data from reliable sources to serve as proof of the viability of whatever project or endeavor the business seeks financing for.

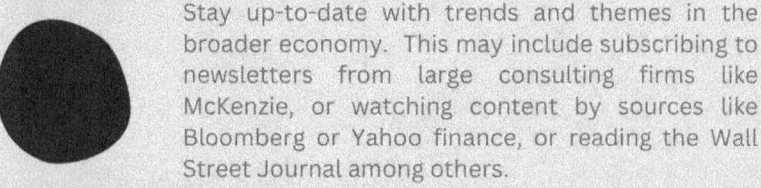 Stay up-to-date with trends and themes in the broader economy. This may include subscribing to newsletters from large consulting firms like McKenzie, or watching content by sources like Bloomberg or Yahoo finance, or reading the Wall Street Journal among others.

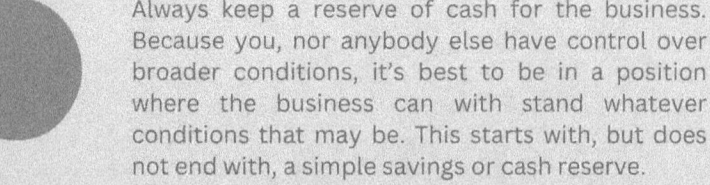 Always keep a reserve of cash for the business. Because you, nor anybody else have control over broader conditions, it's best to be in a position where the business can with stand whatever conditions that may be. This starts with, but does not end with, a simple savings or cash reserve.

Conclusion

To conclude, Capital is a fundamental requirement for every business, regardless of its type or size. Whether it's a small local business like a barber shop or a global giant like Walmart, they all need financial resources. The specific amount, timing, and purpose for capital can vary, but the need for it remains consistent. In today's society, most business operations and growth require financial investments. Entrepreneurs and business leaders should be prepared to seek and secure financing to ensure their business's success.

Moreover, there are various options available for businesses to obtain capital, including loans, lines of credit, investments, and grants. Each option has its own advantages and disadvantages, and it is important for business owners to carefully consider which option is the best fit for their specific needs and goals.

It is also crucial for businesses to have a solid financial plan in place to ensure the efficient and effective use of capital. This includes creating a budget, tracking expenses, and regularly reviewing financial statements. With a well-planned financial strategy, businesses can maximize their resources and achieve their objectives.

In addition, businesses should also prioritize building and maintaining strong relationships with their financial partners, including investors, lenders, and stakeholders. By demonstrating transparency, accountability, and a commitment to success, businesses can establish trust and credibility, which can lead to long-term partnerships and growth opportunities.

In summary, while capital is a necessary component of any business, obtaining and managing it effectively requires careful planning and execution. By understanding their financial needs, exploring available options, and building strong relationships, businesses can ensure their financial stability and success in the long run.

Business leaders need to recognize the universal need for capital in every business venture. Whether it's a small enterprise or a large corporation, financial resources are essential. Understanding and mastering the five C's of credit – Character, Capacity, Capital, Collateral, and Conditions – is crucial to position your business for financing approval with favorable terms. By proactively addressing these aspects, you increase your chances of obtaining the capital you need to thrive and grow your business.

www.ingramcontent.com/pod-product-compliance
Lightning Source LLC
Chambersburg PA
CBHW072244170526
45158CB00002BA/1004